The boy who
loved books

by
KAY WINTERS

❧

illustrated by
NANCY CARPENTER

ALADDIN PAPERBACKS
New York London Toronto Sydney

To Marguerite Winters,
who has always loved Lincoln—K. W.

To the Bevill-Giles family,
a family of book lovers—N. C.

Special thanks to Jessica Schulte, a sensitive editor— K. W.

In the wilds of Kentucky, 1809,
a boy was born.
His mother called him Abraham,
his last name Lincoln.
His bed was made from corn husks,
his covers, skins from bears.
His cabin built with logs
from towering trees.

Abe said his first words
in that one-room cabin,
took his first steps
on a hard dirt floor.
A wood fire chased the cold
and cooked corn pone.

The door swung
open
shut
on leather hinges.
A tiny window looked
out
on his world.

When he was two,
his folks packed their few goods,
moved Abe and sister Sarah
to Knob Creek.

The Cumberland Trail
ran close to their new cabin.
Abe saw peddlers, pioneers,
politicians, traders, slaves
pass by.
As Abe grew,
he talked to travelers—
heard where they'd been,
where they were going.
He saw their world was wider
than his own.
His ideas stretched.
His questions rose.
His dreams were stirred.

At school
he worked with numbers
one to ten.
He shaped his letters *A* to *Z*
with a charcoal stick.

He wrote them down,
day in, day out,
in school, at home,

in dust, in snow, on logs of wood.
The letters cast a magic spell.
He *loved* to learn.

His parents
had no schooling.
But when day was done,
the family sat close by the fire,
his mother shared the Bible stories
she knew by heart.
His father spun yarns, told jokes,
and made them laugh.

When Abe was seven,
the family moved again.
The Lincolns set out
one December morning,
their bits and pieces piled
on two stout horses.

They walked and rode
a hundred miles to Indiana.

They crossed the Ohio River
on a makeshift ferry.
Abe helped his father
hack a trail
through forests thick with trees
and tangled vines.
Until at last they came
to land they claimed.

No cabin waited
at Little Pigeon Creek.
Instead a half-faced camp
of branches, twigs, and logs
was where they had to stay.
One side opened wide
to wilderness.

The family kept the woodpile stacked.
The blazing fire
scared off wild animals
that roamed the woods.

Bears growled,
wolves howled,
panthers screamed.
Abe shivered.
Dark was a fearsome time.

Then settlers came to help
the family raise a home.
Now Abe and Sarah
had a loft to call their own.
Abe loved to climb up
to his sleeping place.
But snow and wind
blew through the cabin's cracks.
The outside crept indoors
and iced the walls.

Just once
Abe shot a turkey in the woods.
But not again.
He vowed he would not
take the breath from living things.

When Abe was eight,
he helped his father
clear their land.
He learned to swing an ax
and fell the trees,
but he longed to learn from
books,
go back to school.

When Abe turned nine,
dark days fell upon him.
Milk sickness took his mother
to her grave.
Abe whittled pegs
to put in her pine coffin,
his grief so deep,
he could not speak her name.

A year limped by.
His father went to find a wife.
He brought back a widow
with three children.
Her heart so wide,
she took in Abe and Sarah
as her kin.

And she owned books!
She let Abe read when chores were done.
Once more their house of logs
became a home.

She sent the children
back to school.
Abe wore too-short buckskins
and a raccoon cap.
He drew his letters with a turkey-buzzard quill.
"Abraham Lincoln
his hand and pen
he will be good but
God knows when."

He learned to add,
subtract on planks of wood.
But most of all he loved to read,
win spelling bees,
spin yarns, tell tales.

When school was shut,
Abe hired out to farmers.
His father kept the earnings
for the family.
Abe split rails, dug wells, chopped trees.
But all the while he worked,
he yearned to learn.
To anyone who'd listen
he liked to say, "The things
I want to know are in books."

Once rain leaked
through the cabin roof
and soaked a book he'd borrowed.
For three hot days
Abe pulled stalks of corn
in his friend's field
to pay him back.

When Abe plowed,
a book sat in his back pocket.
At each row's end
he'd take it out and read.
His horse would wait
for him to turn the page.
The neighbors shook their heads
and called him lazy.

They did not understand this bookish boy.
Abe knew he must move on,
out of the wilderness.
Splitting rails and plowing land
was not his dream.

At nineteen
he poled a flatboat
down the river.
Saw people and places
beyond backwoods.
Saw black men, women,
and their children bound in chains.
A sign above their heads read,
AUCTION BLOCK.

A life for sale
like hatchet, ax, or plow?
Abe knew it was unjust
to own another.

New Salem, Illinois, was where Abe settled.
A hundred folk or more lived in this place!
He hired on to run the general store.
Folks liked to tell that once
he overcharged someone six cents,
but "Honest Abe" walked miles to give it back.

Even here, Abe was asked to prove his worth
with brawn, not brains.
The owner of Abe's store set up a wrestling match
against the leader of a wild and rowdy gang.
Reluctantly, Abe took Jack Armstrong on.
Some said that Abe pinned Jack to the floor,
others swore Armstrong beat Abe with a trick.

But when Jack saw Abe's strength, he shook his hand.
And they became close friends in years to come.

By firelight he studied law without a teacher.
Soon he became a lawyer in the courts.
Abe saw that words could free
or jail a man.
He found that words
could change the way folks thought.

When politics began to call his name,
Abe aimed his words at wrongs
he'd like to right.
Friends said that he should run for public office.
He tried for Congress first, and then the Senate.
At last he ran for the highest office in the land.

Abraham Lincoln—
born in a log cabin,
child of the frontier,
head in a book—
elected our sixteenth president!
From the wilderness
to the White House.
He learned the power of words
and used them well.

AUTHOR'S NOTE

Abraham Lincoln was born on the frontier in 1809 to Nancy and Thomas Lincoln. His formal education amounted to less than a single year. Lincoln was encouraged to read by his mother. But when he was nine years old, Nancy died of milk sickness, a disease caused by drinking milk from cows that have eaten poisonous white snakeroot. A year later Thomas brought home a new wife to be stepmother to Abe and his sister, Sarah. To Abe's delight she arrived with books! As he grew into a young adult he saw how powerful words were and he spent hours writing speeches, preparing debates, and practicing his presentations.

In 1842 he married Mary Todd, and they had four boys, Robert, Eddie, Willie, and Tad. Eddie and Willie died in childhood, leaving the Lincolns bereft.

In 1847 Abe began his two-year term in Congress. Then he left politics and focused on his law career. But the states were deeply divided; the slavery issue was simmering. Lincoln could not keep silent. He ran for Senate. He lost twice, but he didn't give up. His words were quoted, his ideas debated, he became nationally known.

In 1860 he was elected the sixteenth president of the United States. He served this country during one of the most chaotic times in our history—the Civil War. During these dark days, he led the struggle to preserve the Union. On January 1, 1863, he issued the Emancipation Proclamation,* which declared that slaves in those areas of the Confederacy still in rebellion were free. Lincoln was reelected in 1864, but on April 14, in 1865, he was shot in Ford's Theater by John Wilkes Booth. Lincoln died the next day. Secretary of War Edwin Stanton said, "Now he belongs to the ages."

Today Lincoln's face shines on our pennies, his figure meditates at the Lincoln Memorial, his words ring out on patriotic occasions. Because of Lincoln we have a *United* States, and no citizen is owned by another. Abraham Lincoln's love of books, the ideas they stirred, and his way with words kept our nation on the path to freedom. We travel on.

*The Emancipation Proclamation is not a law in the usual sense of the word. It was not passed by Congress. It was a presidential declaration in time of war.

SELECTED BIBLIOGRAPHY

Donald, David Herbert. *Lincoln.* New York: Simon & Schuster, 1996.

Freedman, Russell. *Lincoln, A Photobiography.* New York: Clarion, 1987.

Harness, Cheryl. *Young Abe Lincoln, The Frontier Days, 1809–1837.* Washington, D.C.: National Geographic, 1996.

Sandburg, Carl. *Abraham Lincoln: The Prairie Years and the War Years.* New York: Harcourt Brace, 1926.

Warren, Louis. *Lincoln's Youth.* Indiana: Indiana Historical Society, 1991.

ALADDIN PAPERBACKS
An imprint of Simon & Schuster Children's Publishing Division
1230 Avenue of the Americas, New York, NY 10020
Text copyright © 2003 by Kay Winters
Illustrations copyright © 2003 by Nancy Carpenter
All rights reserved, including the right of
reproduction in whole or in part in any form.
ALADDIN PAPERBACKS and colophon are
registered trademarks of Simon & Schuster, Inc.
Also available in a Simon & Schuster
Books for Young Readers hardcover edition.
Designed by Lee Wade
The text of this book was set in Spectrum.
The illustrations for this book were rendered in oil paint on canvas.
Manufactured in China 0522 SCP
First Aladdin Paperbacks edition January 2006
20 19 18

The Library of Congress has cataloged
the hardcover edition as follows:
Winters, Kay.
Abe Lincoln: the boy who loved books / by Kay Winters ;
illustrated by Nancy Carpenter.—1st ed.
ISBN-13: 978-0-689-82554-5 (hc.)
ISBN-10: 0-689-82554-4 (hc.)
1. Lincoln, Abraham, 1809–1865—Juvenile literature. 2. Lincoln,
Abraham, 1809–1865—Childhood and youth—Juvenile literature.
3. Lincoln, Abraham, 1809–1865—Views on books and reading—
Juvenile literature. 4. Presidents—United States—Biography—
Juvenile literature. [1. Lincoln, Abraham, 1809–1865—Childhood
and youth. 2. Presidents.] I. Carpenter, Nancy ill. II. Title
E457.905.W56 2002
973.7'092—dc21
[B] 00-052223
ISBN-13: 978-1-4169-1268-2 (pbk.)
ISBN-10: 1-4169-1268-1 (pbk.)